BLUE RIBBON

Miniature Quilts

Chitra

Introduction

Sunrises are beautiful no matter where you may live. With their promise of a new day, they greet us with the freshness of morning and the enchanting songs of birds. But have you ever viewed a beach sunrise at the crack of dawn? What an awesome experience!

Similarly, we have viewed many lovely quilts but believe the Blue Ribbon miniatures are the most incredible. These award-winning quilts have been chosen from the annual Miniatures from the Heart Contest by Chitra Publications. They are truly works of art. These quilters carefully selected their fabric while displaying their talent and exquisite handiwork. With so many outstanding quilts in the contest, it was hard to limit this book to just eight. Yet the selection offers you an assortment of techniques and styles. We're sure you're going to appreciate the splendor found on the following pages and find inspiration to stitch along with some of the very best. So start today and create a masterpiece that will be absolutely breathtaking!

The editorial team, from left to right: Pam Broe, Debra Feece, Debbie Hearn, Jack Braunstein

31143007411003
746.4604 Blu
Blue ribbon miniature quilts.

First Printing: 2005

Library of Congress Cataloging-in-Publication Data

Blue ribbon miniature quilts / from the editors of Miniature quilts magazine.
   p. cm.
 ISBN 1-885588-63-1 (pbk.)
1. Patchwork--Patterns. 2. Quilting--Patterns.
 3. Miniature quilts. I. Miniature quilts.
TT835.B5128 2005
746.46'041--dc22
               2004020903

Edited by: Deborah Hearn
Design and Illustrations: Brenda Pytlik
Photography: Van Zandbergen Photography, Brackney, Pennsylvania, unless otherwise indicated

Our Mission Statement

We publish quality quilting magazines and books that recognize, promote, and inspire self-expression. We are dedicated to serving our customers with respect, kindness, and efficiency.
www.QuiltTownUSA.com • (800)628-8244

Contents

Autumn
Whisper
by Shoko Ferguson

4

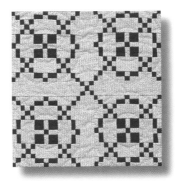

Burgoyne
Revisited
by Lisa Benson

10

With a "Littler"
Help from
My Friends
by Alberta Dalke

12

Safe
Harbor
by Pat Kuhns

14

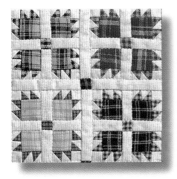

Pleased with
Plaid Paws
by Tina Witherell

16

Mini Geese
in the Barn
by Julie Kato

18

Almost
Amish Baskets
by Diane Becka

20

Golden
Melody
by Cheryl Kagen

22

3

Quilt Size: *28" square*

Materials

- Assorted red print scraps ranging from light to dark
- Assorted light print scraps
- 1/2 yard beige print for the background
- Assorted autumn colored print scraps for the Broken Dishes blocks. Include yellows, golds, greens, rusts, oranges, and reds.
- Assorted green prints for the stems and leaves
- 1/4 yard light green print for the inner border
- 1/4 yard medium green print for the outer border
- 1/4 yard dark green print for the outer border
- 1/4 yard gold print for the outer border
- 1/2 yard purple print for the outer border and binding
- 30" square of backing fabric
- 30" square of thin batting
- Small amount of polyester stuffing

Cutting

Appliqué pieces (page 9) are full size and do not include a seam allowance. Make a template from each pattern piece. Trace around the templates on the right side of the fabric and add a 1/8" turn-under allowance as you cut the pieces out. All other dimensions include a 1/4" seam allowance.

For the quilt center:

- Cut 4: 3/4" x 8 1/4" bias strips, assorted red prints, for the basket handles
- Cut 24: 1 7/8" squares, assorted red prints, then cut them in half diagonally to yield 48 large triangles
- Cut 24: 1 1/8" squares, assorted red prints, then cut them in half diagonally to yield 48 small triangles
- Cut 48: 1 1/4" squares, assorted red prints
- Cut 12: 1 3/8" squares, assorted light prints, then cut them in half diagonally to yield 24 triangles
- Cut 48: 1 1/4" squares, assorted light prints
- Cut 24: 3/4" squares, assorted light prints
- Cut 1: 3 3/8" square, beige background print
- Cut 4: 2 1/2" x 4 1/2" rectangles, beige background print
- Cut 2: 7 1/8" squares, beige background print, then cut them in half diagonally to yield 4 triangles

For the Broken Dishes border:

- Cut 144: 2 1/4" squares, assorted green, yellow, gold, and red prints
  NOTE: *Cut approximately 54 assorted greens, 22 assorted yellows, and 68 assorted reds. These numbers can vary according to your preference and available scraps but should total 144.*

For the light corner triangles:

- Cut 2: 6 7/8" squares, beige background print, then cut them in half diagonally to yield 4 triangles
- Cut 8: 1 1/2" x 13" strips, beige background print
- Cut 8: 2 1/2" x 13" strips, light green print

For the outer border:

- Cut 24: 1 1/4" squares, dark green print
- Cut 48: 1 1/4" x 2 1/4" strips, dark green print
- Cut 2: 1 7/8" squares, dark green print, then cut them in half diagonally to yield 4 corner triangles
- Cut 1: 1 1/4" x 8" strip, gold print
- Cut 48: 1 1/4" x 2" strips, gold print
- Cut 12: 2 3/8" squares, gold print, then cut them in quarters diagonally to yield 48 triangles
- Cut 1: 1 1/4" x 8" strip, medium green print
- Cut 48: 1 1/4" x 2 1/4" strips, medium green print
- Cut 20: 1 1/4" squares, medium green print
- Cut 1: 1 1/4" x 8" strip, purple print
- Cut 40: 1 1/4" x 2" strips, purple print
- Cut 8: 1 1/4" x 2 3/4" strips, purple print
- Cut 12: 2 3/8" squares,

(continued on page)

"Autumn Whisper" *by Shoko Ferguson of Clinton, Maryland, is the 1999 Miniatures from the Heart Contest Best of Show winner. Expertly crafted and imaginative are just two ways to describe Shoko's work.*

purple print, then cut them in quarters diagonally to yield 48 triangles

For the appliqué:

- Cut 41: flowers, assorted red, yellow and pink prints
- Cut 41: circles, assorted red, purple, and yellow prints, for the flower centers
- Cut 1: 3/8" x 4" bias strip, green print, for the stems
- Cut 4: leaves, one green print
- Cut 8: 3/8" x 10" bias strips, assorted green prints, for the stems
- Cut 36: circles, assorted gold and orange prints, for the berries
- Cut 112: leaves, assorted green prints

Also:

- Cut 4: 1 1/4" x 40" strips, purple print, for the binding

Directions

For the quilt center:

1. Draw a diagonal line from corner to corner on the wrong side of each 1 1/4" light print square.

2. Place a marked square on a 1 1/4" red print square, right sides together. Stitch 1/4" away from the drawn line on both sides. Make 48.

3. Cut the squares on the drawn lines to yield 96 pieced squares. Press the seam allowances toward the red prints then trim the allowances to 1/8".

4. Trim each pieced square to 3/4" square.

5. Lay out 2 pieced squares, a 3/4" light print square and a small red print triangle. Stitch them together, as shown, to make a pieced unit. Make 24. Set them aside.

6. Lay out 2 pieced squares and a small red print triangle. Stitch them together to make a pieced unit, as shown. Make 24.

7. Lay out a pieced unit from each group and a light print triangle. Stitch them together to make a pieced triangle, as shown. Stitch a large red print triangle to the pieced triangle to make a block. Make 24.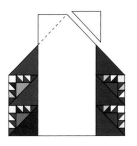

8. Stitch 2 large red print triangles to a block to make a pieced triangle, as shown. Make 4.

9. Stitch pieced triangles to the sides of the 3 3/8" beige background print square to make the center square, as shown. Set it aside.

10. Stitch 2 blocks and a la red print triangle together to make a pieced unit. Make a reverse pieced unit. Make 4 of each, as shown.

11. Stitch a pieced unit an reverse pieced unit to a 2 1/ 4 1/2" beige background print r angle, aligning the bottom ed Make 4. Trim the top corners of e beige print rectangle, as shown

12. Stitch 2 large red print triangles to a block to make a pieced triangle, as shown. Make 4.

13. Lay out the center squ rectangle units and pieced tr gles. Join them, as shown, to m the Basket unit. Set it aside.

. Fold a beige background print
ingle in half to find the center. On
: bottom edge, measure 1 1/4"
m the center on both sides and
ike a mark in the seam allow-
ce.

. Press a 3/4" x 8 1/4" red
nt bias strip into thirds, as
own. Trim 1/8" from each
ig raw edge.

. Pin a pressed bias strip
the triangle for the handle, cen-
ing the ends of the bias strip on
: marks. Appliqué it in place,
erring to the quilt photo on page
as necessary. Make 4.

. Stitch the handle units to the
isket unit to make the quilt center.
m it to 12 1/2" square.

oken Dishes section:

otice the Broken Dishes sections
the quilt in the photo. The quilt-
aker used assorted greens in each
ock for the center of the long side

*of each section. As she worked
toward the outside, she used yellows and golds with greens, then
reds with yellows and golds, then
reds with reds. Refer to the photo as
you make the blocks.*

1. Draw diagonal lines from corner
to corner on the wrong side of 72 of
the 2 1/4" print squares.

2. Place a marked square on an
unmarked 2 1/4" print square, right
sides together. Stitch 1/4"
away from one drawn line
on both sides, as shown.

3. Cut the square on both drawn
lines to yield 4 pieced triangles.
Press the seam allowanc-
es toward the darker
side. Trim the seam
allowances to 1/8".

4. Make pieced triangles from the
remaining 2 1/4" print squares,
combining the colors as described
earlier. Set aside 48; including 8
made with a red triangle and a
green triangle and 8 made with
assorted reds only.

5. From the remaining pieced triangles, stitch 2 together to make a
Broken Dishes block. Make 120.

6. Lay out 30 Broken Dishes blocks
and 12 pieced triangles in 6 rows, as
shown. Using the pieced triangles
you set aside, place 2 red/green
pieced triangles at the ends of the
longest row and 2 red/red pieced triangles forming the shortest row.
Refer to the quilt photo for color

placement. Stitch the blocks and
pieced triangles into rows and join
the rows. Make 4.

7. Stitch these sections to the sides
of the quilt center. Set it aside.

For the light corner triangles:

1. Stitch a 1 1/2" x 13" beige
background print strip to a 2 1/2"
x 13" light green print strip, right
sides together along their length.
Make 8.

2. Center and stitch a beige background print triangle to the light
green side of a pieced
strip, backstitching
1/4" from the corner.
In the same manner,
stitch a pieced strip to
the remaining short
side of the triangle.

3. Miter the corners.

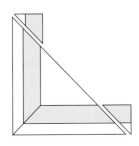

4. Trim the strips even with the
edge of the triangle to make a large
pieced triangle. Make 4.

5. Stitch the large pieced triangles
to the sides of the quilt.

For the outer pieced border:

NOTE: *The measurement of your quilt center should be 24 1/2" square, including seam allowances. The finished measurement of the long side of each border unit you will make in the following steps should be 4". You may wish to make a practice border unit before making all of them. Adjust the seam allowances as necessary to achieve this measurement.*

1. Stitch a 1 1/4" dark green print square to a 1 1/4" x 2" gold print strip. Stop at the 1/4" seamline, as shown, and backstitch.

2. Stitch a 1 1/4" x 2" gold print strip to the adjacent side of the dark green print square in the same manner. Miter the corner to make a pieced square, as shown. Make 24. Set them aside.

3. Stitch a purple print triangle to a 1 1/4" x 2 1/4" dark green print strip. Stitch a purple print triangle to a 1 1/4" x 2 1/4" dark green print strip, reversing the direction, as shown. Make 24 of each. Trim the green print strips even with the purple print triangles to make pieced triangles.

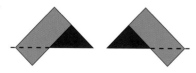

4. Stitch pieced triangles to adjacent sides of a pieced square to complete a Border Triangle A, as shown. Make 24. Set them aside.

5. Make a pieced square, as before, using a 1 1/4" medium green print square and two 1 1/4" x 2" purple print strips. Make 20.

6. Make 24 of each pieced triangle, as before, using the gold print triangles and 1 1/4" x 2 1/4" medium green print strips. Set 4 of each aside for the corner units.

7. Stitch 2 pieced triangles to adjacent sides of a pieced square to complete a Border Triangle B, as shown. Make 20.

8. Lay out 6 Border Triangle A's and 5 Border Triangle B's, as shown. Join them to make a border. Make 4.

9. Stitch the borders to the sides of the quilt. Set it aside.

10. Stitch a 1 1/4" x 8" gold print strip between a 1 1/4" x 8" medium green print strip and a 1 1/4" x 8" purple print strip. Cut four 1 7/8" sections from the pieced strip, as shown.

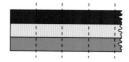

11. Stitch 1 1/4" x 2 3/4" purple print strips to opposite sides of one section, as shown.

12. Center and stitch a dark green corner triangle to the unit. Trim the purple strips even with the edges of the triangle.

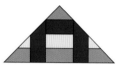

13. Stitch one of each pieced triangle set aside earlier to a unit to make a corner triangle. Make 4.

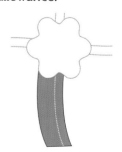

14. Stitch the corner triangles to the corners of the quilt.

For the Appliqué:

1. Using a pencil and a light box or a brightly lit window, lightly trace the Center Block Appliqué Design on the center square.

2. Cut the 3/8" x 4" green print bias strip into four 1" pieces. Lay long edge of a 1" bias stem along marked stem line, right side down, with the strip covering the other marked line. Stitch it by hand to the background square with a 1/4" seam allowance.

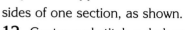

Autumn Whisper

Fold the strip over the stitching
d appliqué the remaining long
lge to the background square,
rning the edge under as you stitch.
epeat for the remaining stems.

Appliqué a red flower in the cen-
r of the square, covering the ends
the stems. Appliqué the 4 green
int leaves.

Referring to the quilt photo,
ppliqué a berry circle covering the
maining end of one stem. NOTE:
*hen you have stitched almost all
e way around the circle, take a
nall piece of polyester stuffing
d insert it through the unstitched
ea. Finish stitching the circle.
epeat with 11 more berry circles
d flower centers to complete the
nter block.*

Appliqué 3 flowers inside the
andle of each basket. Appliqué a

circle in the center of each flower,
lightly padding them, as before.

7. Trace the Border Appliqué Design
on the light green section on one
side of a corner placing the dashed
line at the mitered corner. Flip the
pattern and trace it on the adjacent
side of the same corner. Repeat for
the remaining corners.

8. Prepare the 3/8" x 10" assorted
green print bias strips for the stems
as before.

9. Appliqué the pieces in the following order: short stems, long stems,
leaves, flowers, yellow circles for the
flower centers, and gold and orange
circles for the berries. Lightly stuff
the flower centers and berries.

10. Finish the quilt, according to
the *General Directions* using the
1 1/4" x 40" purple print strips for
the binding.

*Full-Size Border
Appliqué Design
for Autmn Whisper*

*Full-Size Center
Block Appliqué Design
for Autmn Whisper*

Burgoyne Revisisted

Quilt Size: *18 3/4" x 23 1/4"*
Block Size: *3 3/4" square*

Materials

- 3/4 yard red
- 1 1/8 yards beige
- 21" x 26" piece of backing fabric
- 21" x 26" piece of thin batting

Cutting

Cut all strips on the lengthwise grain. All dimensions include a 1/4" seam allowance.

- Cut 16: 3/4" x 25" strips, red
- Cut 8: 1" x 25" strips, red
- Cut 4: 1 1/4" x 25" strips, red, for the binding
- Cut 16: 3/4" x 25" strips, beige
- Cut 4: 1" x 25" strips, beige
- Cut 14: 1" x 4 1/4" strips, beige, for the sashing
- Cut 17: 1 1/4" x 4 1/4" strips, beige, for the sashing
- Cut 4: 2 3/4" x 22" strips, beige, for the border
- Cut 96: 1" x 1 1/4" rectangles, beige
- Cut 48: 1 1/4" x 1 3/4" rectangles, beige

Directions

Press all seams toward the red fabric then trim them to 1/8".

1. Stitch a 3/4" x 25" red strip to a 3/4" x 25" beige strip, right sides together along their length. Make 4 pieced strips.

2. Cut one hundred-four 3/4" sections from the pieced strips, as shown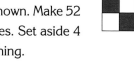

3. Stitch two 3/4" sections together to make a Four Patch block, as shown. Make 52 Four Patches. Set aside 4 for the sashing.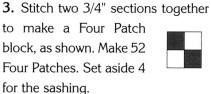

4. Stitch a 3/4" x 25" beige strip between two 3/4" x 25" red strips. Make 4.

5. Cut one hundred-eighteen 3/4" sections from the pieced strips.

6. Stitch a 3/4" x 25" red strip between two 3/4" x 25" beige strips. Make 2.

7. Cut sixty-four 3/4" slices from the pieced strips.

8. Piece 54 Nine Patches using 2 sections with red ends and one section with beige ends, as shown. Six will be used in the sashing.

9. Piece 10 sashing units using one section with red ends and one section with beige ends, as shown.

10. Stitch a 3/4" x 25" beige strip between two 1" x 25" red strips. Make 4.

11. Cut forty-eight 3/4" sections and twenty-four 1" sections from the pieced strips.

12. Stitch a 3/4" x 25" red strip between two 1" x 25" beige strips. Make 2.

13. Cut sixty 3/4" sections from the pieced strips.

14. Make 12 large Nine Patches using two 1" sections with red ends and one 3/4" section with beige ends, as shown.

15. Make 48 side units using o[ ] 3/4" section with red ends and one 3/4" section with beige ends, as shown.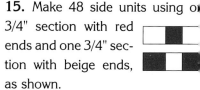

16. Lay out a block using 4 Fo[ ] Patches, 4 Nine Patches, 4 si[ ] units, one large Nine Patch, fo[ ] 1 1/4" x 1 3/4" beige rectangles, a[ ] eight 1" x 1 1/4" beige rectangle[ ] as shown. Stitch the units into row[ ] then join the rows. Make 12 block[ ]

Assembly

1. Referring to the photo, lay o[ ] the blocks, sashing strips, 4 Fo[ ] Patches, 6 Nine Patches, and sas[ ] ing units. Stitch the units into row[ ] Join the rows.

2. Measure the length of the qui[ ] Trim two 2 3/4" x 22" beige strips [ ] that measurement and stitch the[ ] to long sides of the quilt.

3. Measure the width of the qui[ ] including the borders. Trim th[ ] remaining 2 3/4" x 22" beige strip[ ] to that measurement and stitc[ ] them to the remaining sides of th[ ] quilt.

4. Finish the quilt according to th[ ] *General Directions* using the 1 1/4 x 25" red strips for the binding.

"Burgoyne Revisited" *won First Place in the Strip-Pieced category of the 1992 Miniatures from the Heart Contest. Made by Lisa Benson of Erie, Pennsylvania, with over 1,300 pieces, it's no surprise she also won the ribbon for the most pieces.*

With a "Littler" Help from My Friends

Quilt Size: *16 1/2" square*
Block Size: *2" square*

Materials

- Assorted green prints, each at least 2" square
- Assorted dark prints in a variety of colors, each at least 2" square
- Assorted light prints, each at least 2" square
- Fat eighth (10" x 18") dark green print for the binding
- 19" square of backing fabric
- 19" square of thin batting
- Paper for the foundations

Cutting

Fabric for foundation piecing will be cut as you stitch the blocks. Each piece must be at least 1/4" larger on all sides than the section it will cover. All other dimensions include a 1/4" seam allowance.

- Cut 5: 1 1/4" x 18" strips, dark green print, for the binding

Directions

The foundation pattern is full-size and does not include a seam allowance. Follow the foundation-piecing instructions in the General Directions *to piece the blocks.*

1. Trace the pattern 64 times on the foundation paper, transferring all lines and numbers. Cut each one out on the outer line.

2. Piece each foundation in numerical order using the following fabrics in these positions:

For each of 4 foundations:

Use green prints in all the positions.

For each of 24 foundations:

1 through 6 - green prints
7 - light print
8 through 14 - green prints
15 - light prints
16 through 22 - green prints
23 - light print
24 through 30 - green prints
31 - light print
32 through 41 - green prints

For each of 36 foundations:

1, 2, 3, 4, 5 - assorted dark prints
6, 7, 8, 9 - assorted light prints
10, 11, 12, 13 - assorted dark prints
14, 15, 16, 17 - assorted light prints
18, 19, 20, 21 - assorted dark prints
22, 23, 24, 25 - assorted light prints
26, 27, 28, 29 - assorted dark prints
30, 31, 32, 33 - assorted light prints
34 through 41 - assorted dark prints

3. Trim the fabric 1/4" beyond the edges of each foundation.

4. Referring to the quilt photo, lay out the blocks in 8 rows of 8.

5. Stitch the blocks into rows and join the rows. Trim the seam allowances to 1/8" after pressing.

6. Gently remove the paper foundations.

7. Finish the quilt, according to the *General Directions,* using the 1 1/4" x 18" dark green print strips for the binding.

Full-Size Foundation Pattern for With a "Littler" Help from My Friends

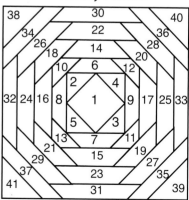

"With a 'Littler' Help from My Friends" *by Alberta Dalke of St. Petersburg, Florida,
won First Place in the Foundation-Pieced category of the 2001 Miniatures
from the Heart Contest. Alberta says that she first made this design in
full size and had to beg greens from her friends so she named that quilt
"With a Little Help from My Friends." With the leftovers from the large
quilt she made this mini, thus the title of her little quilt.*

Safe Harbor

Quilt Size: *16" square*
Block Size: *3 1/2" square*

Materials

- 1/2 yard navy print
- 1/3 yard light blue print
- 1/4 yard white
- 18" square of backing fabric
- 18" square of thin batting
- Paper for the foundations

Cutting

Patterns A, B, and C (page 29) are full size and include a 1/4" seam allowance. Fabric for foundation piecing will be cut as you stitch the blocks. Each piece should be at least 1/2" larger on all sides than the section it will cover. Refer to the General Directions as needed. All other dimensions include a 1/4" seam allowance.

- Cut 4: A, light blue print
- Cut 4: B, light blue print
- Cut 5: C, light blue print
- Cut 4: 5/8" x 13" strips, light blue print
- Cut 4: 3/4" x 13" strips, white
- Cut 4: 2 1/2" x 17" strips, navy print
- Cut 2: 1 1/4" x 40" strips, navy print, for the binding

Directions

Foundation patterns (page 29) are full size and do not include a seam allowance. Follow the foundation-piecing instructions in the General Directions *to piece the foundations.*

1. Trace the patterns on foundation paper, transferring all lines and numbers. Cut each one out on the outer line. Make 32 each of Foundations 1 and 2, 16 of Foundation 3, and 12 of Foundation 4.

2. Piece each foundation in numerical order using the following fabrics in these positions:

For each Foundation 1:
- 1 - navy print
- 2 - light blue print
- 3, 4 - white
- 5 - navy print
- 6 - light blue print

For each Foundation 2:
- 1 - navy print
- 2 - light blue print
- 3, 4 - white
- 5 - light blue print
- 6 - navy print

For each Foundation 3:

Use navy print for the shaded sections and light blue print for the unshaded ones. Start piecing in the center and work toward each end.

For each Foundation 4:
- 1 - navy print
- 2, 3, 4, 5 - light blue print

3. Trim the fabric 1/4" beyond the edges of each foundation.

4. Join a Foundation 1 and a Foundation 2 to make a quarter circle. Make 32.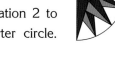

5. Join 2 quarter circles to make a half circle. Make 14.

6. Join 2 half circles to make a circle. Make 5.

7. Appliqué the curved edge of a light blue print A to a quarter circle to make a corner block. Make 4.

8. Appliqué the curved edge of light blue print B to a half circle to make a side block. Make 4.

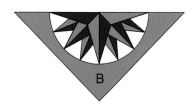

9. Reverse appliqué the curved edge of a light blue C to a full circle to complete a block. Make 5.

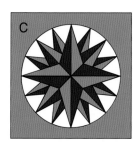

Assembly

1. Referring to the quilt photo, lay out the blocks, side blocks, corner blocks, Foundation 3's and Foundation 4's.

(continued on page 29)

14

"Safe Harbor" *by Pat Kuhns of Lincoln, Nebraska, was awarded*
Best of Show in the 2003 Miniatures from the Heart Contest.
Pat says that she made her first quilt in 1997. She started by
going to the library to learn as much as she could about
quilting, since she didn't come from a family of quilters.

Quilt Size: *14 1/2" square*
Block Size: *1 3/4" square*

Materials

- Assorted plaid scraps
- 1/2 yard beige
- 17" square of backing fabric
- 17" square of thin batting

Cutting

Dimensions include a 1/4" seam allowance.

For each of 13 blocks:

- Cut 2: 2 1/2" squares, one plaid
- Cut 4: 1" squares, matching or coordinating plaid

For the border blocks:

- Cut 22: 2 1/2" squares, assorted plaids
- Cut 44: 1" squares, assorted plaids

From the beige:

- Cut 48: 2 1/2" squares
- Cut 96: 3/4" squares
- Cut 52: 3/4" x 1 1/4" strips
- Cut 36: 3/4" x 2 1/4" strips
- Cut 4: 2 1/2" x 3 1/4" rectangles
- Cut 4: 2 1/2" squares
- Cut 2: 3 3/4" squares, then cut them in half diagonally to yield 4 inner corner triangles
- Cut 4: 1" x 12" strips
- Cut 10: 2 3/8" squares, then cut them in quarters diagonally to yield 40 setting triangles

- Cut 40: 1 1/4" x 1 3/4" rectangles
- Cut 2: 2 3/4" squares, then cut them in half diagonally to yield 4 outer corner triangles
- Cut 2: 1 1/4" x 40" strips for the binding

Also:

- Cut 13: 3/4" squares, plaid, to match or coordinate with the blocks
- Cut 24: 3/4" squares, assorted plaids, for the cornerstones

Directions

Trim the seam allowances to 1/8" after pressing.

1. Draw diagonal lines from corner to corner on the wrong side of each 2 1/2" beige square. Draw vertical and horizontal lines through the centers.

For each block:

1. Place a marked beige square on a 2 1/2" plaid square, right sides together. Stitch 1/4" away from both sides of the diagonal lines, as shown. Make 2 using matching plaids.

2. Cut the squares on the drawn lines to yield 16 pieced squares. Press the seam allowances toward the plaid. Trim the pieced squares to 3/4"

3. Stitch 2 pieced squares together, as shown, and stitch the unit to one side of a 1" plaid square.

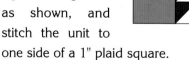

4. Stitch 2 pieced squares and a 3/4"

beige square together, as shown, and stitch the unit to the plaid square to complete a Paw Unit. Make 4 matching Paw Units.

5. Lay out 4 Paw Units, four 3/4" 1 1/4" beige strips and a 3/4" plaid square. Stitch them into rows and join the rows to complete a block. Make 13. Set them aside.

Assembly

1. Referring to the Assembly Diagram (page 30), lay out the blocks point, the 3/4" x 2 1/4" beige strips and 3/4" plaid cornerstone squares. Place four 2 1/2" beige squares at the 2 1/2" x 3 1/4" beige rectangles at the ends of the rows.

2. Stitch the blocks, sashings, cornerstones, squares, and rectangles into rows.

3. Stitch the beige inner corner angles to the corners of the quilt.

4. Trim the quilt 3/4" beyond outer points of the outermost cornerstones.

5. Center and stitch a 1" x

(continued on page 3

"Pleased with Plaid Paws" *by Tina Witherell of Pendleton, Oregon, won First Place in the Pieced Traditional Quilt category of the 2003 Miniatures from the Heart Contest. Tina has been quilting for about 25 years and has always strived to use an exact 1/4" seam allowance. She says that if the piecing is accurate everything will fit together easily.*

Mini Geese in the Barn

Quilt Size: *19 1/2" square*
Block Size: *2" square*

Materials

- Fat eighth (10" x 18") red print; or a piece at least 12" square
- Assorted brown prints totaling at least 5/8 yard
- Assorted light prints totaling at least 5/8 yard
- Assorted prints, such as teal, blue, purple, rust, pink, each at least 1 1/2" square and totaling 5/8 yard
- 3/4 yard beige print
- 1/4 yard dark blue print for the binding
- 22" square of backing fabric
- 22" square of thin batting
- Paper for the foundations

Cutting

Fabric for foundation piecing will be precut for most positions. Each piece should be at least 1/4" larger on all sides than the section it will cover. All other dimensions include a 1/4" seam allowance.

For the Log Cabin Blocks:

- Cut 36: 1" squares, red print
- Cut 3/4"-wide strips, assorted brown prints, at least 12"-long for each of 36 blocks
- Cut 3/4"-wide strips, assorted light prints, at least 11"-long for each of 36 blocks

For the Flying Geese rows:

- Cut 336: 1" x 1 1/2" rectangles, assorted prints

For the Cornerstones:

- Cut 49: 1 1/4" squares, assorted prints

Also:

- Cut 434: 1 3/8" squares, beige print, then cut them in half diagonally to yield 868 triangles
- Cut 3: 1 1/4" x 30" strips, dark blue print, for the binding.

Directions

Foundation patterns (page 30) are full size and do no[t] include a seam allowance. Follow the foundation-piec[]ing instructions in the General Directions *to piece th[e] blocks.*

1. Trace the patterns on the foundation paper, transfe[r]ring all lines and numbers or shading. Make 36 Log Cab[in] blocks, 84 Flying Geese rows, and 49 Cornerstones. Cu[t] each foundation out on the outer line.

2. Piece each foundation in numerical order using th[e] following fabrics in these positions:

For the Log Cabin blocks:

Center - 1" squares, red print
1, 2 - 3/4"-wide strips, light prints
3, 4 - 3/4"-wide strips, brown prints
5, 6 - 3/4"-wide strips, light prints
7, 8 - 3/4"-wide strips, brown prints
9, 10 - 3/4"-wide strips, light prints
11, 12 - 3/4"-wide strips, brown prints

For the Flying Geese rows:

Shaded sections -assorted 1" x 1 1/2" print rectangles
Unshaded sections - beige print triangles

For the Cornerstones:

1 - 1 1/4" square, print
2, 3, 4, 5 - triangles, beige print

3. Trim the fabrics 1/4" beyond the edges of each foundation.

Assembly

1. Lay out 6 Log Cabin blocks and 7 Flying Geese row[s] as shown. Join them to make a row. Make 4.

2. Lay out 6 Log Cabin blocks and 7 Flying Geese row[s] as shown. Join them to make a row. Make 2

(continued on page 3[0])

"Mini Geese in the Barn" *by Julie Kato of Sammamish, Washington, won a ribbon for the Best New Entry in the 2002 Miniatures from the Heart Contest. Julie says she started seriously quilting about 11 years ago and she has met so many wonderful people through her guilds. She uses foundation piecing whenever she can and loves reproduction fabrics.*

Quilt Size: *16 1/2" square*
Block Size: *1 7/8" square*

Materials

- 5" square each of 25 bright hand-dyed fabrics
- 5/8 yard black
- 1/8 yard purple
- 1/8 yard red
- 1/2 yard green
- 19" square of backing fabric
- 19" square of thin batting

Cutting

The appliqué pattern (page 31) is full size and does not include a turn-under allowance. Make a template from the pattern. Trace around the template on the right side of the fabric and add a 1/8" to 3/16" turn-under allowance when cutting the fabric pieces out. All other dimensions include a 1/4" seam allowance.

For each of 25 Basket blocks:
- Cut 1: 2" square, bright fabric
- Cut 1: 2 1/2" square, same bright
- Cut 1: 1 1/4" square, same bright, then cut it in half diagonally to yield 2 triangles

Also:
- Cut 25: 2" squares, black
- Cut 25: 2 1/2" squares, black
- Cut 13: 1 5/8" squares, black, then cut them in half diagonally to yield 26 small

triangles. You will use 25.
- Cut 50: 7/8" x 1 5/8" strips, black
- Cut 3: 4 1/2" squares, black, then cut them in quarters diagonally to yield 12 setting triangles
- Cut 2: 2 3/4" squares, black, then cut them in half diagonally to yield 4 corner triangles
- Cut 4: 2" x 18" strips, black, for the border
- Cut 2: 1 1/4" x 40" strips, black, for the binding
- Cut 64: 7/8" x 2 3/8" strips, purple, for the sashings
- Cut 40: 7/8" squares, red, for the cornerstones

For the appliqué:
- Cut 1: 1/2"-wide bias strip, green, for the vine, to total 60" when joined
- Cut 104: leaves, green

Directions

Trim the seam allowances to 1/8" after pressing.

For each Basket block:

1. Draw a diagonal line from corner to corner on the wrong side of each 2" black square.

2. Place a marked 2" black square on a 2" bright square, right sides together. Stitch 1/4" away from the drawn line on both sides.

3. Cut the squares on the draw line to yield 2 large pieced square. You will use one. Press the sea allowance toward the black.

4. Draw diagonal lines from corn to corner on the wrong side of ea 2 1/2" black square. Draw horizontal and vertical lines through the centers, as shown.

5. Place a marked 2 1/2" bla square on a 2 1/2" same brig square, right sides together. Stitch 1/4" away from both sides of the diagonal lines, as shown.

6. Cut the squares on the draw lines to yield 8 small pieced square You will use 7. Press the seam allow ances toward the black.

7. Join 3 small pieced squares, and stitch the row to a large pieced square, as shown.

8. Join 4 small pieced squares ar stitch the row to the large piec square, as shown.

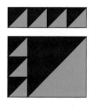

9. Stitch a small bright triangle a 7/8" x 1 5/8" black strip to mal

(continued on page 3

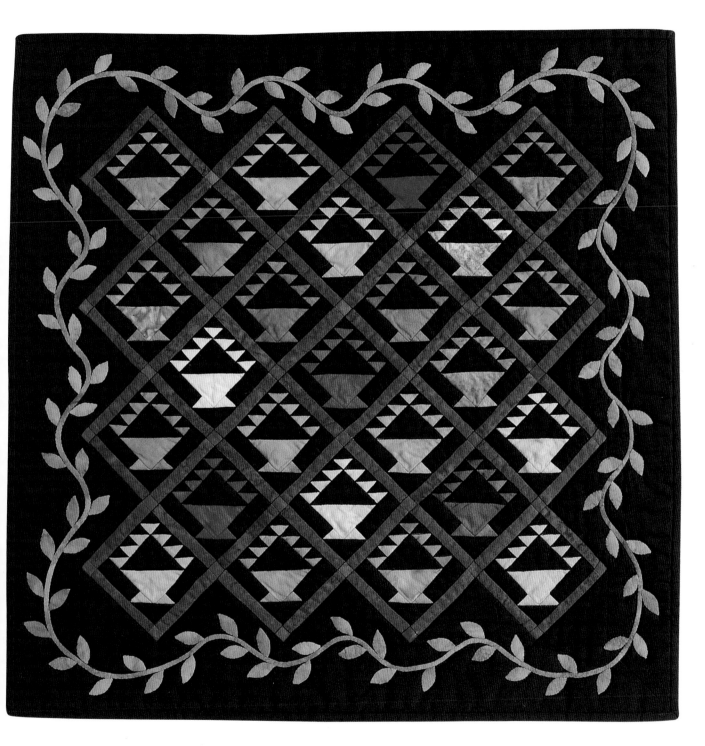

"Almost Amish Baskets" *is a work of precision by Diane Becka*
of North Bend, Washington. Diane used a different batik for each basket
to show off a large number of them from her collection. This quilt won
first place in the Combination Pieced and Appliquéd Quilt category
of the 2002 Miniatures from the Heart Contest.

Golden Melody

Quilt Size: *23" square*

Materials

- 5/8 yard white
- 5/8 yard mottled blue
- 1/3 yard light gray print
- 1/3 yard mottled gray
- 1/3 yard yellow
- Assorted yellow and gold print scraps for the tulip appliqués
- 8" square of gold print for the flower centers
- 1/3 yard green for the stems
- Assorted green print scraps for the leaves
- Scrap of butterfly print fabric with 3 butterflies ranging in size from 1/2" to 7/8" across (optional)
- 25" square of backing fabric
- 25" square of thin batting
- Paper for the foundations
- Loop turner for the stems

Cutting

Appliqué pieces (pages 27 and 28) are full size and do not include a seam allowance. Make a template from each pattern. Trace around the appliqué templates on the right side of the fabric and add a 1/8" to 3/16" turn-under allowance when cutting the pieces out. All other dimensions include a 1/4" seam allowance. You have the choice of a traditional piecing method or foundation piecing
for the small triangle sections of the quilt. If you would like to use foundation piecing, do not cut pieces D through I. Fabric for foundation piecing can be cut as you stitch the units. Each piece must be at least 1/2" larger on all sides than the section it will cover.

- Cut 1: A, white
- Cut 8: E, white
- Cut 8: J, white
- Cut 4: 2 1/2" x 25" strips, white
- Cut 8: B, mottled blue; or cut four 2 1/4" squares, then cut them in half diagonally to yield 8 triangles
- Cut 4: L, mottled blue; or cut two 5 5/8" squares, then cut them in half diagonally to yield 4 corner triangles
- Cut 116: G, mottled blue; or cut twenty-nine 2 1/8" squares, then cut them in quarters diagonally to yield 116 triangles
- Cut 1"-wide bias strips, mottled blue, to total at least 96" when joined for the binding NOTE: *Golden Melody is finished with a narrow single fold bias binding.*
- Cut 8: C, light gray print
- Cut 112: G, light gray print; or cut twenty-eight 2 1/8" squares, then cut them in quarters diagonally to yield 112 triangles
- Cut 8: D, yellow

- Cut 8: H, yellow
- Cut 8: K, yellow
- Cut 4: 7/8" x 21" strips, yellow
- Cut 8: F, mottled gray
- Cut 8: I, mottled gray
- Cut 8: IR, mottled gray
- Cut 4: 7/8" x 21" strips, mottled gray

For the appliqué:

- Cut 28: M, assorted yellow and gold prints
- Cut 28: MR, assorted yellow and gold prints
- Cut 36: N, assorted yellow and gold prints
- Cut 36: NR, assorted yellow and gold prints
- Cut 64: O, gold print
- Cut 96: P, assorted green prints
- Cut 11: 1 1/4" x 10" bias strips, green

Directions

1. Stitch 4 mottled blue B's to t[   ] white A to make a pieced square, [   ] shown.

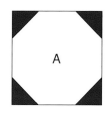

2. Stitch 2 light gray print C's to [   ] mottled blue B to make a side un[   ] Make 4.

(continued on page 2[ ]

When Cheryl Kagen of West Seneca, New York, challenged herself to make a
miniature quilt entirely by hand, she created this blue and yellow medallion
style mini. **"Golden Melody"** became the Best of Show winner in the 2000
Miniatures From the Heart Contest. The tulip appliqué was designed by
Deborah L. White and appeared in her book No Big Deal: Mastering
the Art of Miniature Quiltmaking (That Patchwork Place, 1997).

3. Stitch the side units to the pieced square to make a pieced octagon. Set it aside.

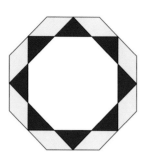

NOTE: *If you would like to foundation piece the following units, see page 26.*

4. Stitch a white E between a yellow D and a mottled gray F to make a pieced unit, as shown. Make 8.

5. Lay out 5 mottled blue G's and 4 light gray print G's. Stitch them together to make a pieced strip, as shown. Make 8.

6. Stitch a pieced strip between a yellow H and a pieced unit, as shown. Make 8.

7. Stitch a mottled gray I and a mottled gray IR to a unit, as shown.

Stop stitching at the dot on the yellow H and backstitch.

8. Miter the seam between the I and IR, stitching only between the dots and backstitching at each one to secure the seams. Make 8.

9. Stitch a unit to each side of the pieced octagon, stitching only between the dots and backstitching at each one to secure the seams.

10. Stitch the seams between the units, stopping at the outer dots and backstitching. The unit now looks like an 8-point star.

11. Set the white J's into the 8-Point Star unit, as shown.

12. Stitch a yellow K to ea side of the unit, stitching or between the dots and backstitc ing to secure the seams. Stitch t seams between the yellow K's miter the corners.

13. Stitch the mottled blue to the unit to complete the qu center.

For the appliqué:

1. Using the patterns (on pag 27 and 28) as a placement guid lightly mark the design lines on th A, E and J sections of the qu Refer to the quilt photo as nece sary. Set the quilt aside.

2. Fold a 1 1/4" x 10" green bias strip in half, right side in. Stitch 1/8" away from the folded edge, as shown.

3. Trim the long raw edges 1/8" beyond the stitc

ing line. Using a loop turner, turn the strip right side out to make a tube. Make 11.

4. Cut the appropriate lengths from the bias tubes for the stems. Appliqué them to the quilt center on the traced stem lines, adjusting each tube so the seam is centered on the underneath side.

5. For each flower on the A and E sections of the quilt, appliqué the upper edges of a gold print O. Appliqué a gold or yellow print MR then a gold or yellow print M, covering the inner edge of the gold print O.

6. Appliqué an O, an MR, and an M on each seamline between the E's, covering the ends of the stems.

7. For each flower on the J sections, appliqué an O, an NR, and N.

8. Appliqué the assorted green print P's (leaves) on the quilt center.

To make the Pieced Border:
Follow the directions below for a pieced middle border or use the foundation on page 26.

For traditional piecing:
1. Lay out 19 blue G's and 20 light gray print G's. Join them to make a pieced border. Measure the length of the pieced border between the seam allowances on the longest edge, as shown. It should measure 17 5/8". Adjust a few seams, if necessary, to make it that length. Make 4.

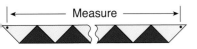
Measure

For foundation piecing:
Follow the foundation-piecing in-structions in the General Directions *to piece the borders. Use the foun-dation on page 26.*

1. Trace the border patterns on the foundation paper, joining them at the dots to make a complete Border Foundation for one side of the quilt. Be sure to transfer all lines, shading, and dots. Make 4. Cut each one out on the outer line.

2. Stitch each foundation using mottled blue in the shaded sec-tions and light gray print in the remaining ones.

3. Trim the fabric 1/4" beyond the edges of each foundation.

Assembly

1. Center and stitch a pieced bor-der between a 7/8" x 21" gray strip and a 7/8" x 21" yellow strip, keep-ing the blue G's against the gray strip.

2. Center and stitch the pieced strip to a 2 1/2" x 25" white strip, placing the yellow strip against the white strip. Refer to the quilt photo, as necessary. Make 4.

3. Center and stitch the borders to the sides of the quilt. Start and stop stitching 1/4" from the edges and backstitch.

4. Miter each corner referring to the *General Directions.*

5. With a pencil, draw a soft curve on each corner of the quilt, as shown.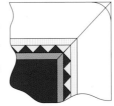

6. Referring to the quilt photo, appliqué stems, leaves, and tulips on each corner.

7. Appliqué butterflies, cut from the butterfly print fabric, on the border, as desired.

NOTE: *For the H pieces, the quilt-maker used the design on pattern piece H (on page 27) and on sec-tion 10 of the foundation pattern (on page 26) alternately on her quilt.*

8. Layer the backing, batting, and quilt top and quilt as desired. Use the quilting designs provided on the pattern pieces and on page 28.

9. Stitch the bias strips together with diagonal seams to make a long binding strip. Press one long edge 1/4" toward the wrong side. Trim the pressed under edge to 1/8".

10. Leaving approximately 4" of binding free, stitch the unpressed edge of the bias binding to the quilt, right sides together and raw edges aligned. Stop within 4" of the starting point. Fold the ends back along the edge of the quilt so that the folded edges meet and trim them 1/2" from the folds. Join the ends with a diagonal seam and finish stitching the binding to the quilt.

11. Trim the edge of the quilt as you fold the binding over it, leaving enough seam allowance to fill the binding. Hand stitch the binding to the back of the quilt, covering the stitching line.

(continued on page 26)

Foundation Piecing Golden Melody

Some of the pieced sections in Golden Melody can be stitched on foundations.

Directions

Foundation patterns are full size and do not include a seam allowance. Follow the foundation piecing instructions in the General Directions *to piece the units.*

1. Trace the foundation pattern 8 times on the paper, transferring all lines and numbers. Cut each one out on the outer line.

2. Piece each foundation in numerical order using the following fabrics in these positions:

    1, 3, 5, 7 and 9 -mottled blue

    2, 4, 6, 8 - light gray print

10 - yellow

11 - mottled gray

12 - white

13 - yellow

14 and 15 - mottled gray NOTE: *Stop stitching pieces 14 and 15 at the dot on the foundation and backstitch. Stitch the pieces together to make a mitered seam, stopping at the dot and backstitching.*

3. Trim the fabric 1/4" beyond the edges of the foundation.

4. Stitch the foundation pieced units to the pieced octagon as described in Step 9 of the quilt pattern.

5. Gently remove the foundation papers after the quilt top has been assembled.

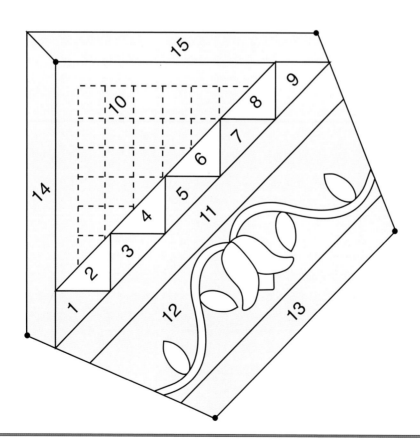

Full-Size Patterns for Golden Melody
(more patterns on page 28)

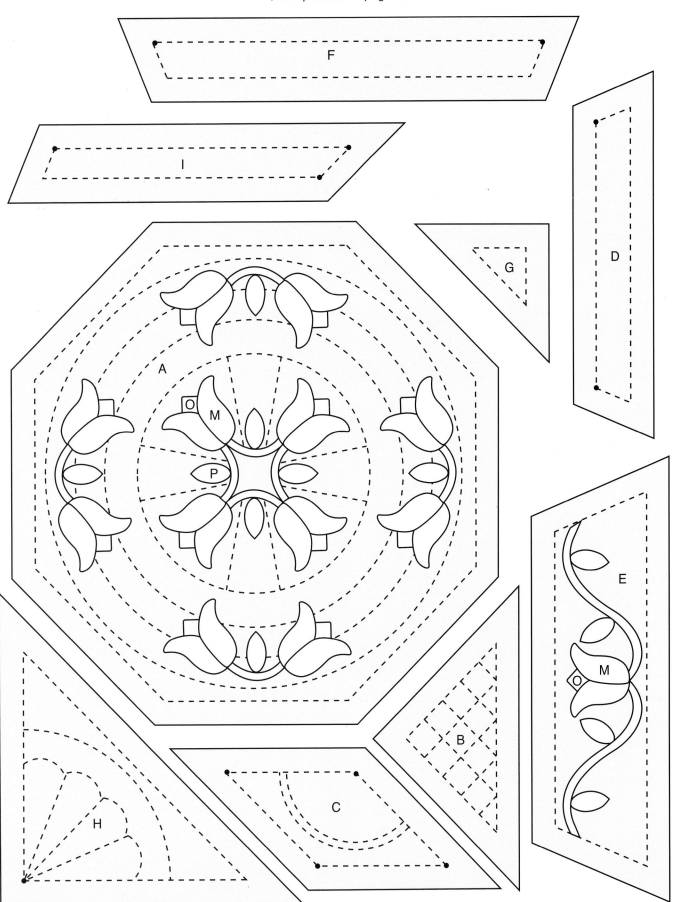

Golden Melody *(continued from page 27)*

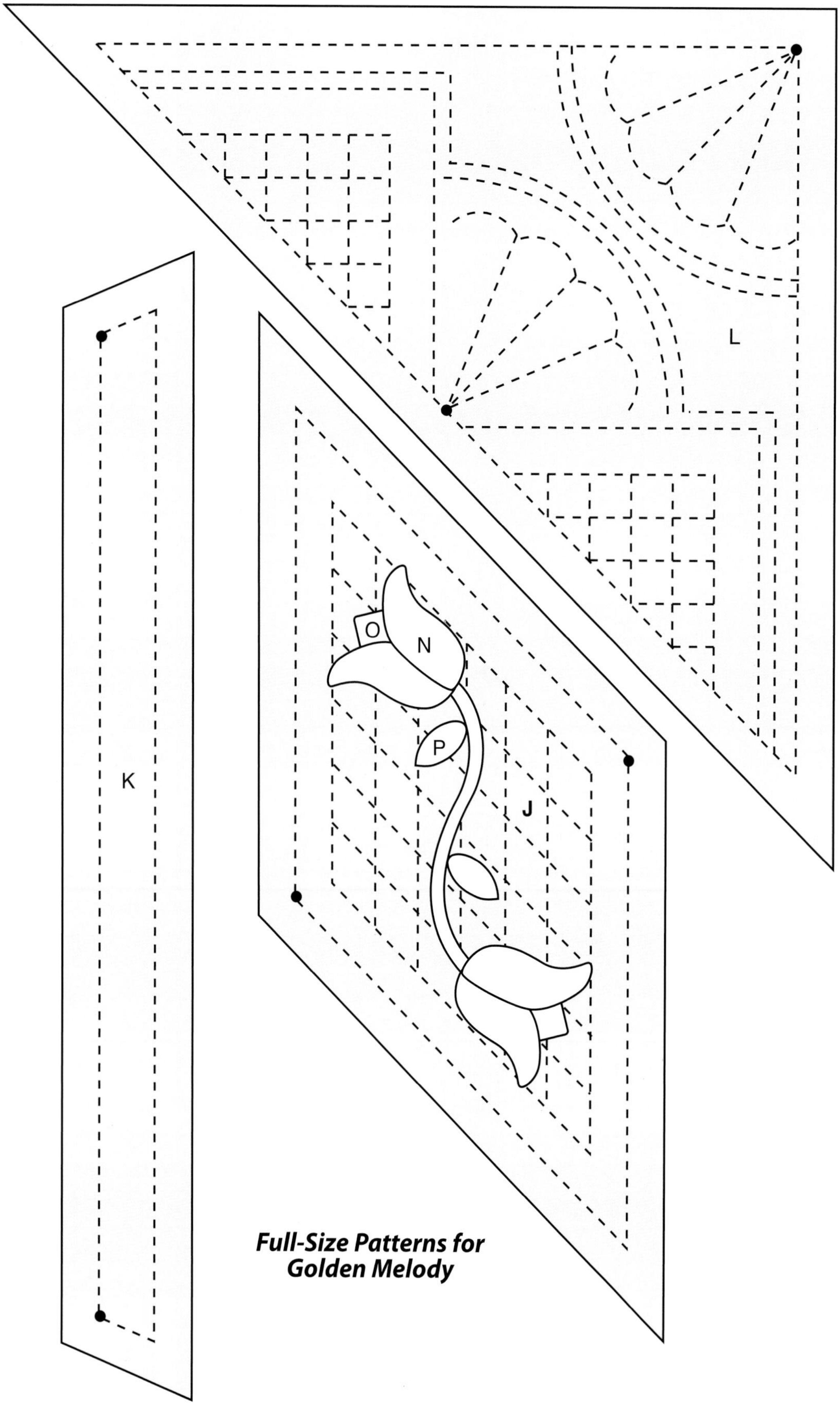

Full-Size Patterns for
Golden Melody

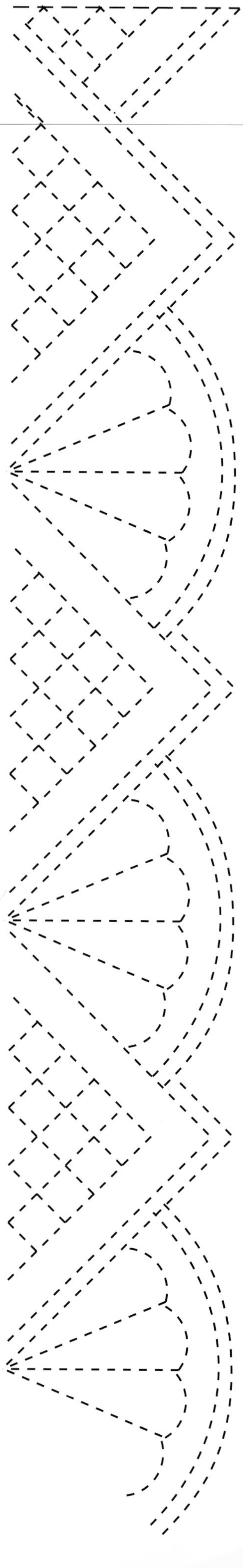

L

K

O

N

P

J

1/2 Quilting Design for the Outer Border for Golden Melody

28

Safe Harbor *(continued from page 14)*

2. Stitch the units into diagonal rows and join the rows.

3. Trim the Foundation 4's to straighten the edges of the quilt.

4. Measure the length of the quilt. Trim two 3/4" x 13" white strips to that measurement. Stitch them to opposite sides of the quilt.

5. Measure the width of the quilt, including the borders. Trim the remaining 3/4" x 13" white strips to that measurement. Stitch them to the remaining sides of the quilt.

6. In the same manner, trim the 5/8" x 13" light blue print strips to fit and stitch them to the quilt.

7. Trim the 2 1/2" x 17" navy print strips to fit and stitch them to the quilt.

8. Finish the quilt, according to the *General Directions,* using the 1 1/4" x 40" navy print strips for the binding.

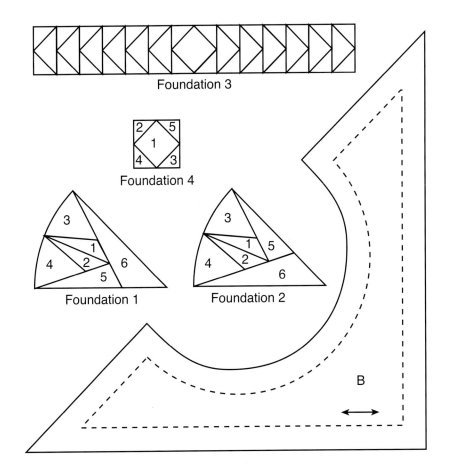

Foundation 3

Foundation 4

Foundation 1

Foundation 2

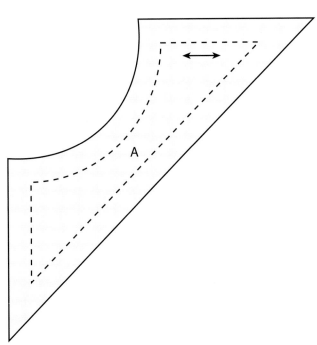

B

Full-Size Foundations and Patterns for Safe Harbor

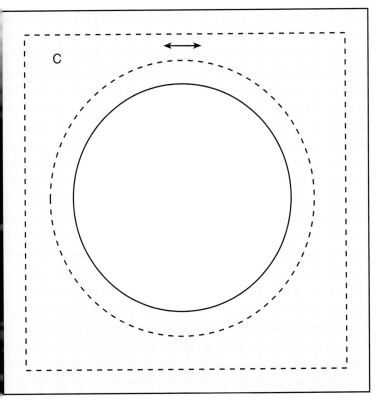

C

A

Pleased with Plaid Paws (continued from page 16)

beige strip to each side of the quilt. Start, stop, and backstitch 1/4" from the edges.

6. Miter each corner.

For the pieced borders:

1. In the same manner as before, make 44 Paw Units.

2. Lay out a row of 11 Paw Units on point, as shown, with 10 beige setting triangles along one long side of the row and ten 1 1/4" x 1 3/4" beige rectangles along the opposite long side.

3. Stitch the Paw Units, triangles, and rectangles into diagonal sections. Join the sections to make a pieced border. Make 4.

4. Center and stitch the borders to the quilt and miter the corners.

5. Stitch beige outer corner triangles to the corners.

6. Trim the edges of the quilt 7/8" beyond the outermost points of the Paw Units.

7. Finish the quilt according to the *General Directions,* using the 1 1/4" x 40" beige strips for the binding.

Assembly Diagram

Mini Geese in the Barn (continued from page 18)

3. Lay out 6 Flying Geese rows and 7 Cornerstones, as shown. Stitch them together to make a sashing row. Make 4.

4. Lay out 6 Flying Geese rows and 7 Cornerstones, as shown. Stitch them together to make a sashing row. Make 3.

5. Referring to the quilt photo on page 19, lay out the block rows and sashing rows. Stitch them together.

6. Gently remove the paper foundations.

7. Finish the quilt, according to the *General Directions,* using the 1 1/4" x 30" dark blue print strips for the binding.

Full-Size Foundation Patterns for Mini Geese in the Barn

Cornerstone

Log Cabin Block

Flying Geese Row

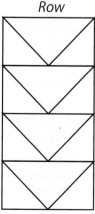

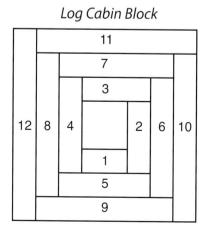

a pieced strip. Make another pieced strip, reversing the direction of the triangle, as shown.

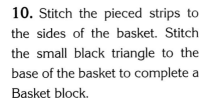

10. Stitch the pieced strips to the sides of the basket. Stitch the small black triangle to the base of the basket to complete a Basket block.

Assembly

1. Referring to the Assembly Diagram, lay out the Basket blocks, the 7/8" red cornerstones, the 7/8" x 2 3/8" purple sashing strips, and the black setting and corner triangles.

2. Stitch the cornerstones and sashing strips into strips.

3. Stitch the sashing strips and Basket blocks into rows.

4. Stitch a pieced strip to each pieced row. Stitch the setting and corner triangles to the rows.

5. Center and stitch the 2" x 18" black strips to the sides of the quilt. Start, stop and backstitch 1/4" from the edges.

6. Miter each corner.

7. Fold the green bias strip in thirds right side out, and press, as shown.

8. Referring to the quilt photo, appliqué the vine to the quilt top.

9. Appliqué the green leaves, approximately 26 per quilt side.

10. Finish the quilt, according to the *General Directions*, using the 1 1/4" x 40" black strips for the binding.

Appliqué Leaf Pattern

Assembly Diagram

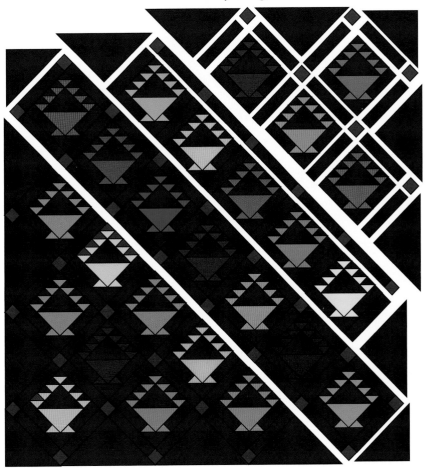

General Directions

About the Patterns
Read through the pattern directions before cutting fabric for the quilt.

Fabrics
Yardage is based on fabric with a useable width of 40". We recommend using 100% cotton fabrics. We suggest washing your fabrics before using them.

Marking Fabric
Always test marking tools for removability. We suggest using silver or white marking tools for dark fabrics and fine-line pencils for light fabrics.

Templates
Template patterns are full size and, unless otherwise noted, include a 1/4" seam allowance. Trace patterns on clear plastic.

Pieced Patterns
For machine piecing, make templates with the seam allowance. Trace around the templates on the right side of the fabric. For hand piecing, make templates without the seam allowance. Trace templates on the wrong side of the fabric, flipping all directional (asymmetrical) templates before tracing, and add a 1/4" seam allowance as you cut the fabric pieces out.

Appliqué Patterns
A seam allowance is not included on appliqué patterns. The solid line is the sewing line. Make a template and lightly trace around it on the right side of the fabric. For needleturn appliqué, add a 1/8" to 3/16" turn-under allowance when cutting the fabric pieces out. Clip inside curves almost to the pencil line so they will turn under smoothly as you stitch.

Needleturn Appliqué
Pin an appliqué piece in position on the background fabric. Using thread to match the appliqué piece, thread a needle with a 15" to 18" length and knot one end. Using your needle, turn under a short section of the allowance on the appliqué piece, and bring the needle from the wrong side of the background fabric up through the fold on the marked line of the appliqué piece. Push the needle through the background fabric, catching a few threads, and come back up through the background fabric and the appliqué piece on the marked line close to the first stitch. Use the point of the needle to turn under and smooth the allowance, and make another stitch in the same way. Continue needleturning and stitching until the piece is completely sewn to the background fabric. To reduce bulk, do not turn under the allowance or stitch where one appliqué piece will be overlapped by another.

Foundation-pieced Patterns
Place fabric pieces on the unmarked side of the foundation and stitch on the marked side. Center the first piece, right side up, over position 1 on the unmarked side of the foundation. Hold the foundation up to a light to make sure that the raw edges of the fabric extend at least 1/2" beyond the seamline on all sides. Hold this first piece in place with a small dab of glue or a pin, if desired. Place the fabric for position 2 on the first piece, right sides together. Turn the foundation over and sew on the line between 1 and 2, extending the stitching past the beginning and end of the line by a few stitches on both ends. Trim the seam allowance to 1/8". Fold the position 2 piece back, right side up, and press. Continue adding pieces to the foundation in the same manner until all positions are covered and the block is complete. Trim the fabric 1/4" beyond the edges of each foundation.

To avoid disturbing the stitches, do not remove the paper until the blocks have been stitched together and the borders have been added, unless instructed to remove them sooner in the pattern. The pieces will be perforated from the stitching and can be gently pulled free. Use tweezers to carefully remove small sections of the paper, if necessary.

Hand Piecing
Use a thin, short needle (sharp) to ensure a flat seam. Begin with a knot and continue with a small, even running stitch, backstitching every 3-4 stitches. Stitch directly on the marked line from point to point, not edge to edge. Finish with 2 or 3 small backstitches before cutting the thread.

Machine Sewing
Set the stitch length to 12 stitches per inch. Stitch pieces together from edge to edge unless directed to do otherwise in the pattern. When directions call for you to start or stop stitching 1/4" from the edges, as for set-in pieces, backstitch to secure the seam.

FINISHING
Marking Quilting Designs
Simple designs can be cut from adhesive-backed shelf paper. They'll stick and re-stick several times. Masking tape can be used to mark grids. Remove the tape when you're not quilting to avoid leaving a sticky residue. Mark lightly with pencils; thick lines that won't go away really stand out on a small quilt.

Batting
Use a thin batting. Layer the quilt sandwich as follows: backing, wrong side up, batting; quilt top, right side up. Baste or pin the layers together.

Quilting
Very small quilts can be lap-quilted without a hoop. Larger ones can be quilted in a hoop or small frame. Use a short, thin needle (between) and small stitches that will be in scale with the little quilt. Thread the needle with a single strand of thread and knot one end. Insert the needle through the quilt top and batting (not the backing) 1/2" away from where you want to begin quilting. Gently pull the thread to pop the knot through the top and bury it in the batting. Quilt as desired.

Binding
For most straight-edged miniature quilts, single-fold binding is an attractive, durable, and easy finish. NOTE: *If your quilt has curved or scalloped edges, binding strips must be cut on the bias of the fabric. Sew the binding strips together with diagonal seams; trim and press the seams open.*

Trim one end of the strip at a 45° angle. Press one long edge of the binding strip 1/4" toward the wrong side. Starting with the trimmed end, position the binding strip, right sides together, on the quilt top, aligning the raw edge of the binding with the bottom edge of the quilt top. Leaving approximately 2" of the binding strip free, and beginning at least 3" from one corner, stitch the binding to the bottom of the quilt with a 1/4" seam allowance, measuring from the edge of the binding and quilt top.

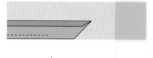

When you reach a corner, stop stitching exactly 1/4" from the edge of the quilt top. Backstitch, clip the threads, and remove the quilt from the machine. Fold the binding up and away, creating a 45° angle, as shown.

Fold the binding down, as shown, and begin stitching at the edge.

Continue stitching around the quilt to within 2" of the starting point. Lay the binding flat against the quilt, overlapping the beginning end. Open the pressed edge on each end, and fold the end of the binding at a 45° angle against the angle on the beginning end of the binding. Finger press the fold.

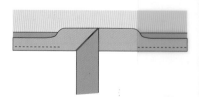

Trim 1/2" beyond the fold line. Place the ends of the binding right sides together, and stitch with a 1/4" seam allowance. Finger press the seam allowance open.

Place the binding flat against the quilt, and finish stitching it to the quilt. Trim the batting and backing even with the edge of the quilt top. Fold the binding over the edge of the quilt, and blindstitch the folded edge to the back, covering the seamline.